Original title:
Lemon Sunrise

Copyright © 2025 Creative Arts Management OÜ
All rights reserved.

Author: Helena Marchant
ISBN HARDBACK: 978-1-80586-408-0
ISBN PAPERBACK: 978-1-80586-880-4

Bright Skies Over Zesty Fields

In a land where colors gleam,
The sun laughs, a citrus dream.
Fields with hues of yellow bright,
Dance beneath the morning light.

Bees are buzzing, quite the show,
Sipping nectar, sweet and low.
Chasing shadows, they take flight,
In this blissful fruit delight.

Morning Nectar and Light

Morning's brew with zest galore,
Sour faces, we implore!
Juicy drops of laughter fall,
Nature's giggles, hear the call.

Chirpy birds in citrus trees,
Making tunes with playful ease.
Each note brings a smile so wide,
As we ride this fruity tide.

A Shimmer of Citrus Joy

Clouds run fast, they start to roll,
Irreverent, like a bowl.
Twirling beams of golden rays,
Join the dance of sunny plays.

Orange slices in the sky,
Flip and bounce, oh my, oh my!
Tickled by the zestful breeze,
Life's a joke, our hearts at ease.

Taste of Dawn's Golden Glow

Awake! The day is bright and bold,
A treasure chest of warmth to hold.
Wake up, friends, let's have some fun,
Banter sweet as morning's sun.

Citrus peels scattered around,
Do the happy dance, unbound!
Laughter sparkles in the air,
As the world begins to care.

The Rise of Golden Nectar

A burst of zest in morning's light,
The world wakes up, what a sight!
With squeaky juice and sticky hands,
Dancing picnics, on the sands.

Birds are chirping, 'What a treat!'
As tangy sunshine hits your feet.
A slice of joy on toast, they say,
Embrace the day, come what may.

Flavorful Horizons

Gleaming globes upon the trees,
A citrus kiss rides on the breeze.
Sipping sunshine from a cup,
With giggles bouncing, up we hop!

Wiggly worms in funny hats,
Join the fun with the dancing cats.
Mimic the squirrels in joyful play,
Unified laughter greets the day.

Dawn's Bright Citrus Dance

Outrageous colors splash the dawn,
As funny hats are thrown upon.
Chasing shadows with a grin,
Spinning round, let the fun begin!

Bright smiles peek through every leaf,
The trees rumor a tale of relief.
Tickling rays on nose and cheek,
A wacky jig, so cute and meek.

Ripe Radiance of Awakening

Awake, awake, to flavors bright,
A party starts at morning light.
With fruity giggles all around,
Zesty peels fall to the ground.

Skip and hop on sidewalks bold,
As sunlight casts a laughter's mold.
Bouncing dreams and citrus fries,
All nature welcomes playful skies.

Citrus Aura at First Light

The sky splashes yellow, not quite ripe,
Chickens strut, plotting their next swipe.
A squirrel swings by on a tangy spree,
Chasing dreams of jam, oh, what a glee!

At dawn's light, the oranges giggle,
While grapefruits bounce, they wiggle and wiggle.
A zesty breeze makes laughter swell,
Who knew dawn could be a carnival?

A Daybreak of Golden Nectar

A toast to the breakfast, it's quite the sight,
With pancakes stacked high, oh what a delight!
The syrup flows like streams of cheer,
Dance around the table, spread the fun near!

Juice drips down, a sticky parade,
With toppings galore, watch out, don't fade!
The toast's getting jealous of all this praise,
As we giggle and munch through the zesty haze.

The Brightness of Citrus Fields

Waking up sprightly, the fields shimmer bright,
With oranges leaning in, what a sight!
A land so zesty, it could make you grin,
Even the bees seem to dance with a spin!

The sun chuckles, bouncing off fruit,
As kittens prance, giving the grass a toot.
Everything's quirky, magnetic, and wild,
This citrus show makes even the grumpiest smile!

Joyful Revelations of the Morning

In the kitchen, chaos tactically brews,
Eggs are wobbling, while mash-ups ensues.
A blender goes rogue, making a splash,
Fruit salad's fight, oh what a clash!

The cat's got a zest for the feathery chase,
While I sip on my smoothie, making a face.
Mornings shine bright like disco in bloom,
What a funny way to wake up the room!

Warm Citrus Threads

A zest-filled glow spills from the sky,
As fruits take flight, oh my, oh my!
The sun wears peels of bright yellow,
While giggling bees dance like a fellow.

Joyful rays tickle the trees,
As squirrels slide down with a tease.
The morning jokes in vibrant zest,
Each citrus laugh is simply the best!

The Golden Embrace of Day

The sun pops up, a jester bold,
With glimmers of sunshine, stories told.
Chasing shadows, it takes a quick run,
Painting the world, oh what fun!

In this glow, even clouds turn bright,
They fluff and puff in pure delight.
With each ray, giggles float high,
As fruits concoct a comical pie!

Orchard Whispers at Dawn

Trees in a huddle, gossiping fruit,
Sharing secrets, all sleek and cute.
A cheeky breeze, oh how it plays,
Sending leaves into a twirly craze.

Every branch holds a joke or two,
Laughter ripples through morning dew.
Silly shadows leap and sway,
In this orchard, fun leads the way!

The Sweetness of Morning Light

Morning breaks with a giggly yawn,
As sweets emerge from slumber's dawn.
With rays that tickle, smile, and wink,
Clouds blow kisses, oh what a link!

Mirth dances on delicate flames,
Pancakes flip, calling your names.
The syrup flows, joy's sticky brand,
In this breakfast nook, all laughter is planned!

Luminous Orchard Awakening

In the grove where laughter flows,
Twisted trees wear silly clothes.
Bouncing fruits in playful cheer,
Whisper secrets for all to hear.

A squirrel winks, a flash of zest,
Chatting leaves, they never rest.
Morning giggles fill the air,
Waking up without a care.

Sunlight's Tangy Invitation

Sunlight bounces on a peel,
Dancing shadows, what a deal!
The world's a stage for citrus jest,
A merry twist, a fruity fest.

Juicy puns on morning's bread,
Pineapples nod their green heads.
A picnic spread, the ants abide,
As orange slices take a ride.

A Radiant Citrus Bloom

Petals chuckle in the breeze,
Humming tunes that tickle knees.
Fluffy clouds play peek-a-boo,
While fuzzy bees hum joy anew.

Citrus cheerleaders line the path,
With pom-poms bright to spark a laugh.
Every bloom a silly grin,
As zestful joy spills from within.

Bright Hues and Dewy Dreams

Dewdrops giggle on the grass,
As butterflies glide with a sass.
Colors spill in hues so bold,
Telling tales in whispers told.

A jam session with the sun,
Chorusing delights, oh what fun!
Every fruit a funny sight,
In the orchard bursting bright.

Sweet Tart Beginnings

Golden glimmers wake the day,
Zesty cheers in bright display.
A squirt of joy from morning's zest,
Who knew breakfast could be such a fest?

Sour notes in laughter's tune,
Citrus giggles greet the noon.
Life's a splash, a tangy bounce,
In every sip, we laugh and flounce.

A Burst of Morning Light

Morning's giggle breaks the dark,
A yellow wink from sunshine's spark.
Bursting forth with smiles on lips,
Even toast does a little flip!

Warm rays dance like silly sprites,
Tickling clouds with unlikely sights.
A bounce, a jig, a cheerful spree,
In the air, joy's melody.

Echoes of Zest in the Air

Whiffs of glee upon the breeze,
A citrus laugh that aims to please.
Silly shadows dress in cheer,
Tickled petals quite sincere.

Bouncing dreams on fuzzy mats,
Sunshine wriggles, how it chats!
Every leaf is in on the joke,
Nature giggles, little strokes.

Dawn's Yellow Promise

Bright rays bloom with cheeky wishes,
Sipping sunshine, swimming fishes.
Cheerful skies wear yellow hats,
Even squirrels dance with sprightly chats!

Morning's wink, a playful tease,
With each beam, the world to please.
Laughter tumbles like a stream,
In this dawn, we wink and beam.

Juicy Daybreak

Morning light spills like juice,
Waking up with a goofy moose.
Birds chirp in fruity delight,
Dancing around, what a sight!

Pancakes stacked, syrup on high,
Butterflies flutter, oh my, oh my!
Sipping on a zesty shake,
Wishing I could just be a cake.

Rooster struts with a bright grin,
In the garden, weeds lose to spin.
Grapefruit giggles, oranges roll,
Who knew breakfast could be so whole!

Citrus jokes fill the air,
Lemonade dreams as a pair.
Chasing shadows in the sun,
With a chuckle, the day's begun!

Sunrise Wrapped in Citrus

Golden rays peek through the blinds,
Cheerful laughter in the finds.
Toast pops up, what a surprise,
On it bounces a sweet disguise!

Kiwis juggling, and limes play tag,
In this kitchen, no room for drag.
Scones and muffins join the fun,
A breakfast party for everyone!

Sipping tea with a zestful twist,
Lemon meringue just can't be missed.
Silly smiles float on the steam,
In this moment, life's a dream!

Sunshine spills on the plate,
Fruits are dancing, oh it's fate.
Every bite brings joy profound,
In citrus bliss, we're glory-bound!

Tang of New Beginnings

Awakening feels so grand,
With peelers ready at our hand.
Zesty scents waft, hugs abound,
Time for laughter all around!

Orange slices make us grin,
While the mixer spins and spins.
Fruity chaos paints the day,
Who knew mornings could be play?

Smiles bloom like bright sunflowers,
In this kitchen, joy empowers.
A splash of juice, a wink, a cheer,
Hello, good vibes; goodbye, the drear!

Every citrus twist a tease,
With silly games as we please.
New adventures sweetly rise,
In this world of fruity skies!

The Citrus Awakening

A playful haze begins to spread,
Under the blanket, dreams take thread.
Waking up with a squirt and splash,
In this morning, we're ready to dash!

Grapefruit giggles fill the air,
As laughter pops up here and there.
Sticky fingers, fruity treats,
Chewing sounds our joy repeats.

Jelly jars dance with delight,
Spoonfuls of sunshine feeling right.
A tasty twist, a silly song,
In this citrus world, we belong!

Mimosa cheers echo around,
With bubbles rising, feels profound.
Each sip a promise of pure joy,
In this merry party, oh boy!

Vibrant Citrus Dawn

A yellow orb spills on the ground,
Waking up the world with a sound.
Birds chirp in a fruity delight,
Dancing shadows in morning light.

A splash of zest in the air,
Socks mismatched, a bold fashion flair.
Mimosas spill as we clink our cups,
Who left the peels in such messy heaps?

A Toast to the Morning Glow

The sun pops up like a fizzy drink,
Bright and bubbly, makes you think.
Coffee brews with a twist of fun,
Sips of joy, the day's begun.

Toast to friends with a zestful grin,
Watch out for juice stains on your chin!
Doughnuts in hand, we take a bite,
Laughter and crumbs in the morning light.

Glow of the Morning Orchard

In the orchard where shadows play,
Fruit hangs low in a merry way.
Grab a basket and start to roam,
What a zesty way to feel at home!

Buzzing bees join the morning cheer,
Bumping into branches, oh dear!
Swinging from trees like a joyful jest,
Who knew mornings could be this blessed?

Sun-Kissed and Zesty

A splash of color fills the skies,
Tickled by rays, no need for sighs.
Fruits are dancing in citrus glee,
What a funny way to be free!

Giggles echo, and laughter grows,
The warmth of the sun tickles our toes.
With each bite, the day unfolds,
Crisp and bright, as joy beholds.

Morning's Tart Embrace

A twisty grin on morning's face,
Wakes me up from my soft space.
Jumpy toes on the kitchen floor,
Sipping joy, I crave for more.

Pouring zest in my brew,
Wobbling like a playful zoo.
Sunlight beams through kitchen vie,
Lemon drops in my eye.

Sunlit Citrus Dreams

Sunrise giggles, oh what fun,
Dancing rays, a golden run.
Zesty whirls in cereal bowls,
Brightened days for silly souls.

Squinting at the day's delight,
Color splashes, oh what sight!
Lively fruits in our parade,
Smiling morns that never fade.

Bright Awakening

An orange glow, I start my day,
With wobbly laughs that come to play.
Toast a little with citrus cheer,
Do we hear a giggle near?

Juicy bursts on every bite,
Silly hats for morning light.
A zestful hop, a giggly roll,
That's how we start, that's our goal!

Yellow Glow on the Horizon

A yellow smile peeks over trees,
Whispers of laughter in the breeze.
Wiggly shadows on the lawn,
Sipping sunshine until it's gone.

Jolty waves in the sunny air,
Bouncing splashes everywhere.
Ninja squints, I chase the sun,
Morning giggles, way more fun!

Hues of Citrus on Awakening Skies

In the morn when fruits do glow,
Orange smiles and yellow throw.
Bouncing flavors dance on air,
Sunshine bursts, no time to spare.

Flying frogs in zestful cheer,
Hopping songs, they're drawing near.
A parade of ripe delight,
Serenade the waking light.

Jesters play on branches high,
Tickling grins, oh what a sky!
Citrus laughter fills the breeze,
Whirling joy with silly ease.

Sun-kissed rays with quirky flair,
Fruits in laughter, everywhere.
Mirth of morning, bright and bold,
Awake my heart, let tales be told.

Golden Orchard Awakening

Gold upon the orchard's face,
Sunshine dips in playful grace.
Dancing bees with nectar dreams,
Wiggling toes and lemonade streams.

Twirling squirrels in fitting hats,
Join the jam with jazzing cats.
Fruitful frolics in the morn,
With giggles sprouting, joy is born.

Each spritz a splatter, oh so bright,
Of jiggling jellies in the light.
Fruit shakes tumble, joy ignites,
Morning mischief pure delight.

So grab your cup, let's take a ride,
In this orchard, joy won't hide.
With fruity fun, the day begins,
A toast to laughter, where joy spins!

Whispers of Citrus at Dawn

Whispers tickle in the trees,
Zesty banter on the breeze.
Giggling fruits in morning's cheer,
Bringing forth the day so queer.

Marigold and tangerine,
Bathing in the glow, pristine.
Silly sounds and sunny beams,
Chasing after silly dreams.

Fruits composing silly tunes,
With bouncy beats and twinkling moons.
Hilarity ripe in every bite,
Torching nonsense, pure delight.

Spritz of joy on dewy grass,
Tickling toes as moments pass.
With laughter cracking dawn's embrace,
Citrus whispers, our heart's race.

Zestful Light's Embrace

Zestful beams on morning's face,
Twisting citrus dance with grace.
A goofy grin lights up the skies,
Fruity fun, no need for shy.

Bouncing on the sunny rays,
Juicy mischief, bright displays.
Each sun-kissed drop a silly throne,
Kites of joy in laughter flown.

Bold and bright in yellow coats,
With rollicking fruits and silly notes.
The day awakes with vibrant cheer,
A zesty hug from far and near.

So come, let's laugh, let's tease and play,
In this citrus world, we'll spend the day.
Together, let's embrace the sun,
With every giggle, we have won!

Tangy Whispers of the Day

With a squirt of zest, the morning greets,
A citrus joke that life repeats.
Sunshine giggles, tickles the tree,
Waking all the bees, oh can't you see?

Flavors dance upon the breeze,
Silly birds begin to tease.
Juicy laughter fills the air,
Makes you want to stop and stare.

Shimmering Essence of Morning

The sky's a puddle of bright gold cheer,
Sipping puddles, have no fear.
Clouds giggle, fluffy in their guise,
As the world pops open sleepy eyes.

Wobbly creatures walk in glee,
With sticky hands, they climb a tree.
Flavored mist hangs in the glow,
Bursting with joy, it's quite a show.

Citrusy Embrace of a New Day

Bright orbs of fun tumble from the sky,
Tickling grass, as they bounce high.
Tangy scents swirl and slide,
Making even sloths want to glide.

Freshly squeezed giggles swirl around,
As the day skips joyfully on the ground.
Bumbling bees buzz with a grin,
Who knew mornings could be such a win?

Honeyed Glints of Sunrise

The sun yawns wide, stretching its beams,
Pouring laughter in golden streams.
Waffle clouds stack, fluffy and sweet,
While silly ants dance on tiny feet.

In this cheerful, golden haze,
Nature plays in silly ways.
Bright sparks tickle the day ahead,
With joyful snacks and dreams to spread.

The Day Awakes with Sunlight Spice

The rooster crows with zest so bright,
It wakes the world with pure delight.
Coffee brews in a citrus haze,
Banana peels in a morning craze.

A squirrel dances on the fence,
Wearing shades, it makes no sense.
The sun spills out its golden cheer,
As pancakes flip without a fear.

Butterflies float on laughter's wing,
While toasters pop — what joy they bring!
All mouths smile in breakfast bliss,
As syrup kisses a fruity kiss.

With giggles shared and joy so wide,
The day begins, an orange tide.
Adventure calls with a playful grin,
As sunlight dances — let fun begin!

Citrus Gold in the Morning Air

A jester hops on a sunny slope,
Wearing a hat made of citrus hope.
He juggles fruit with silly flair,
Chasing giggles through morning air.

The toast does a happy little jig,
Claiming it's the breakfast pig!
Jam is ready, a fruity mess,
On a plate of morning happiness!

Juicy smiles drip from each face,
As laughter spills into the space.
The sun shines down, a playful tease,
Turning maple syrup into breeze.

With bright sunbeams and silly pranks,
We toast our happiness in fruit-filled ranks.
Today we'll laugh and dance so tight,
In the golden glow of morning light.

A Daybreak to Savor

A waking world that spins and twirls,
With candy skies and buttered pearls.
The toast leaps up, a morning call,
Setting a scene of joy for all.

Socks mismatched, a day of glee,
Who knew breakfast could be so free?
Fish in hats swim up the stream,
As we all join the birthday theme!

Eggs dance on the frying pan,
Singing loud, they have a plan.
They'll roll off, have a chat,
With pancakes joining in — imagine that!

With every sip of citrus drink,
We laugh, we smile, we hardly think.
A silly start to a joyful race,
Today, let's savor every trace!

Awakening in Zest

The rooster crows with a twist,
A bright yellow kiss, can't resist.
Tea spills as I leap from my bed,
Dreams of tangy toast in my head.

The cat dances with glee,
Chasing sunbeams, oh let it be!
I stumble, I trip on my shoes,
Caught in a game of silly blues.

Outside as the day unfolds,
A quirky world in yellow golds.
Birds chirp jokes in high-pitched flight,
Their antics make the morning bright.

In this burst of cheerful rays,
All the silly worries decay.
Laughter bubbles, joy's delight,
An orange jester in plain sight.

Tangy Light Breaks

Awake! The world is full of cheer,
A citrus scent that draws us near.
Toast pops up with a playful grin,
Getting ready for the fruity spin.

Joyful squirrels start to plot,
A breakfast feast in the backyard lot.
They scurry and skip, such a sight,
Plotting mischief in morning light.

Muffins rise with a giggling sound,
As sticky sweetness spreads around.
Honey drips like a golden stream,
In this bakery of a silly dream.

Sunshine winks from cloudberry skies,
Wiggling and jiggling, it tries.
Each beam tickles plants and toes,
Tickling laughter, goodness grows.

Radiance of the Citrus Sky

The dawn brings a twisty grin,
Joy unfolds like a lemon skin.
I sip my drink, full of zest,
Morning chaos is always the best.

Pancakes flip with flipsy flair,
Strawberry hats on each pair.
The syrup spills like a giggle spree,
Catching laughter like bumblebees.

The sun dips low, stealing the show,
Casting shadows with a funny glow.
A parade of critters, all in line,
Mischievous giggles, oh how they shine!

In nature's circus, we can see,
A happy dance by a honeybee.
Each buzzing joke spins round and round,
In the citrus air, joy is found.

Sunrise in a Grove

The grove wakes up with a chuckle loud,
Fruitful branches bow, feeling proud.
Sunshine tickles every leaf,
As frolicking beings chase disbelief.

A raccoon in a hat, what a sight!
Pushing his luck in the morning light.
He steals an orange, biting down,
Wearing the juice like a crown!

Crickets chirp funny tunes, no doubt,
Joining the fun as they dance about.
The squirrels all join in the act,
Now who could ever find that cracked?

In laughter's grove, joy fully blooms,
Under the canopy, silliness looms.
Unexpected giggles greet the day,
As fruity banter comes out to play.

Morning Citrus Glow

In the kitchen, a fruit on the floor,
A citrus orb rolls, oh what a chore!
It bounced and it hopped like a little sprite,
Chasing it down gave the cat a fright!

The toast popped up, but I'm all a mess,
Juggling my breakfast — oh, what a stress!
Butterflies fly in a sunny ballet,
While I dance around in a comedic display!

Radiant Zest Awakening

A zesty wake-up with squinty eyes,
I sip my drink and let out loud sighs.
A splash of juice spills right on my shirt,
Now I smell fresh, but my fashion's a hurt!

Birds outside chirp a fruity tune,
Near the blender, watch it start to bloom.
Oranges roll like they're on a spree,
I frame a fruit salad and laugh with glee!

Citrus Hues of Dawn

Morning brightens with a citrus grin,
I can't find my glasses, where to begin?
A flash of yellow from the fruit bowl's light,
I swear that orange was just a sight!

Toast does a tango with some jam,
Spreading sweetness – oh what a scam!
I slip on a peel that was sly as a fox,
And tumble right into a box of socks!

Glistening Gold at Daybreak

Gold spills on my plate like a morning caper,
While I'm crafting a breakfast worthy of paper.
But I find the fruit's got a mind of its own,
Rolling away like it's aiming for the throne!

The kettle sings like it's in a band,
While the smoothie makes art – oh so grand!
A mix-up of flavors, a zany delight,
It drips and it dribbles – a colorful sight!

Citrus Dreams in the Sky

Up above, the citrus gleams,
Orange laughter, yellow dreams.
Clouds like peels, so bright and wide,
A juice-filled world, oh what a ride!

A squirrel sip, a parrot's dance,
Fruit loops whirl in a merry prance.
Tasting sunshine on my tongue,
Counting giggles, feeling young.

Mornings burst with zesty highs,
As yellow rays paint azure skies.
Bouncing berries, a playful chase,
In this sphere of silly grace.

So let us chuckle, laugh and play,
In citrus dreams, we shout hooray!
A zesty kiss from dawn's first light,
Our hearts as bright as sun's delight.

Sun-Mellowed Citrus and Bliss

Behold the fruit, a glowing sphere,
Bouncing laughter, oh so dear.
Sweet tangs twirl in morning's bloom,
A citrus giggle, banish gloom!

Juice drops dance on picky tongues,
As silly songs are sweetly sung.
Nature's candy, sun's embrace,
Fruity pranks in this delight space.

The sun gets glowing, starts to tease,
Bright peels shimmer in the breeze.
Round and round, the fun parade,
In this zesty world we've made.

So sip the joy, and let it swirl,
In sun-mellowed bliss, let laughter twirl.
As clouds bounce on like fluffy beans,
We live amidst these fruity dreams.

Zesty Horizons Await

On the horizon, colors pop,
Juicy secrets, never stop.
Teasing rays of bright delight,
Zesty giggles wake the night.

Round and ripe, a twisty game,
Fruity laughter, never tame.
Sunset dances, sweet and bold,
In this wonder, joy unfolds.

Orange halos kiss the ground,
Bouncing citrus joy around!
We play hide and seek with day,
In zesty fields, we laugh and sway.

So let the horizon be our muse,
In these sweet tones, we shall choose.
With peels of sunshine on our face,
Every moment feels like grace.

Awakening in Sun-Drenched Citrus

Awake to fruit, a sunny morn,
With laughter's spark, we are reborn.
Sippin' sunshine, oh how grand,
In this light, we make our stand.

The day unfolds with a zesty cheer,
As playful spirits gather near.
Orange skies, no cloud in sight,
Life's a game when things feel right.

In the orchard, giggles rise,
As citrus dreams fill up the skies.
Swinging low, the branches sway,
We bounce about in bright display.

So let's embrace this sun-drenched bliss,
With every hug, and every kiss.
In the citrus field where laughter grows,
We dance with joy, in silly throes.

Zestful Dawn Chorus

In the kitchen, oh what a scene,
A fruit frenzy, bright and keen.
Squeezed a wedge, made a splash,
My morning drink, a zesty bash!

Roll my eyes at the silly cat,
Who licks and purrs, where's my hat?
A prankster morn with citrus cheer,
Sing with the birds, 'cause fun is here!

Dance with toast, a jam-filled ride,
With a twist and a whirl, I glide.
Coffee brews, the kettle sings,
Funny things are what dawn brings!

Sunlight spills like a citrus wave,
Each giggle bubbles, oh how we crave.
The day is bright, my heart's in flight,
Laughter bubbles in morning's light!

Awakened by the Citrus Light

Alarm clock buzzes, what a shock!
My pillow's clutch, like a tight lock.
Peeling citrus, a squeeze of fun,
Awake, awake! The day's begun!

Muffins rise, they dance with glee,
Pancakes flip like they're on a spree.
Drizzle honey, what a treat,
Citrus zings, can't be beat!

Chasing shadows, socks askew,
Sipping punch, oh what a view!
With every sip, a smile wide,
Citrus dreams, we'll not subside!

As sunbeams tap on windowpanes,
Life's a twist, with joyful gains.
Pull up a chair, join the fun,
Citrusy mornings just begun!

Morning's Refreshing Splash

A splash of zest, a morning cheer,
Squeiltch and splash, the juice is here!
Fruit so bright, it wears a grin,
Each drink is filled with fun within!

Pancakes flop like they've lost their race,
Bacon smiles, it's a sunny place.
Giggles bubble in a steamy brew,
Citrus twist, well, who knew?

The toaster pops with a little song,
I dance along, I can't go wrong.
With orange peels, I make a crown,
What a way to start this town!

Juicy jokes, the fruit parade,
Every bite, more laughter made.
So here we are, with zest to share,
Morning's splash, beyond compare!

Brightness Between the Trees

Beneath the branches, oh what fun,
Squirrels chatter, morning's begun.
Sunshine zings through leaves so fresh,
Nature's giggle, oh what a mesh!

A citrus scent walks in the air,
While birds sing tunes, without a care.
Laughter ripples like a stream,
Bright as sunshine, it's all a dream!

Jumping jests on the wooden floor,
Sticky fingers, fruit galore.
Every joke wants a zesty twist,
Morning moments, too good to miss!

So step outside, where brightness beams,
Among the trees, we're bursting seams.
With every smile, our hearts increase,
In morning's glow, we find our peace!

Bright Slices of Morning

A citrus giggle fills the air,
With yellow hues in my hair,
The sun winks through my curtain's seams,
Awakening all my fruity dreams.

My toast is dancing on the plate,
It knows that breakfast cannot wait,
With zesty hugs and twists of cheer,
Each bite bursts forth, oh so near!

A glass of juice, so boldly bright,
It tickles ribs and sparks delight,
I sip and smile at kitchen sights,
A joyful start to morning lights.

So laugh along with slices sweet,
As sunshine plays a fruity beat,
In every drop, a little fling,
The day begins—let's laugh and sing!

Tangy Light Breaking Through

When dawn arrives with a cheeky grin,
The sky's ablaze, let the fun begin,
A zesty warmth, oh what a tease,
As light sneaks in like a playful breeze.

A bright parade of yellow rays,
They tickle toes and start the plays,
With laughter bubbling, it's clear to see,
Morning's fruits love a jubilee!

Pancakes flipping, syrup's dance,
Sticky fingers, what a chance!
Each bite a burst, a happy surprise,
As giggles slip through morning skies.

So let the tangy joy unfold,
In this bright story, brave and bold,
With chuckles sweet and morning cheer,
Every moment's a treat, so dear!

Sun-Kissed Orchard Dreams

In orchards bright, the sunlight plays,
While fruity secrets fill the maze,
A beaming grin from every pear,
Swings of laughter, everywhere!

With berry hats and citrus shoes,
The trees conspire to spread the blues,
Each rustling leaf, a joke in bloom,
As laughter binds us—sweet perfume!

The pickers dance with basket swings,
Chasing joy as the chirpy sings,
A mishmash of color, sweet and wild,
A scene that makes the grumpiest smile.

So twirl along the orchard's line,
Where sunshine's touch makes hearts align,
In every bite, a dream fulfilled,
With giggles shared and joy distilled!

Daylight's Fruitful Embrace

The day arrives with citrus cheer,
A giggle bright, we're gathered near,
As golden drops of morning dew,
Invite us all to taste the new.

In every corner, tangy fun,
The fruit parade has just begun,
With bouncing smiles and laughter free,
A banquet spread for you and me!

The coffee brews and pancakes swirl,
As morning's charm begins to twirl,
Each slice of toast a happy muse,
While syrup rivers tickle blues.

So let us feast on sunshine's kiss,
A playful start, a daily bliss,
With every giggle, every cheer,
The day unfolds, our hearts sincere!

Sunlit Petals and Citrus Dreams

Beneath the sun, a yellow glow,
A fruit parade puts on a show.
The petals dance with zestful cheer,
While gardeners laugh, they have no fear.

In every sip, a giggle bubbles,
Nature's prank, with citric troubles.
A squirt of juice, oh what a sight,
Citrus capers, pure delight!

The flowers plot with sugar smiles,
As bees buzz by in silly styles.
A sun-kissed world, bright and bold,
With citrus jokes waiting to unfold.

So let us twirl and skip about,
In tangy fun, we laugh and shout.
For every dawn, a chance to play,
In lemon zest, we'll find our way.

Illuminated Citrus Symphony

A morning band with fruity flair,
The citrus drums fill up the air.
With every squeeze, a note so bright,
The world awakes, a funny sight.

Orange slices on a plate,
Dancing jigs that taste just great.
Limes and grapefruits join the tune,
In this orchard, we're over the moon!

The colors burst, a wild parade,
As we all join this citrus charade.
With giggles loud, we raise our glass,
To sunny fun that will not pass.

So gather round, let's make a toast,
To sunny fruits we love the most!
In this bright world, let's laugh and sing,
A symphony of zest, let joy take wing!

Golden Glare at Dawn

Up with the sun, we greet the day,
Golden glimmers lead the way.
With citrus smiles, we start to play,
A breakfast feast, hip-hip-hooray!

Mimosas dance with orange zest,
The breakfast table is at its best.
We giggle as the juice drips down,
On sunny days, we wear the crown.

The sky's ablaze, a bright delight,
With punny jokes that feel just right.
As fruit flies swirl, uplifted cheer,
A golden hour, we hold dear.

So let the laughter echo wide,
With every sip, we're filled with pride.
At dawn's embrace, let's all convene,
In this bright hue, we'll reign supreme!

Citrus Hues of Morning

Morning breaks with playful rays,
Citrus shades ignite the haze.
With giggles bright and laughter loud,
Nature's palette draws a crowd.

A bright mishap, a squirt in jest,
A citrus splash, we're truly blessed.
With painted skies of orange cheer,
We dance and twirl without a fear.

Bees do the cha-cha on each bloom,
While lemons laugh, dispelling gloom.
In every slice, a story's spun,
As we embrace the morning sun.

Let's revel in this zesty show,
With fruity fun, our spirits glow.
In every drop, a hearty scheme,
We chase the dawn, fulfill the dream!

Daybreak's Zesty Whisper

Morning's laughter bursts so bright,
A jester's hat on the sun's height.
With rays like slices, round and bold,
The day's a prankster, truth be told.

Mirth dances in the blazing glow,
As shadows stretch and giggles flow.
Citrusy sparks in the warm air soar,
Who knew the dawn could tease and roar?

The sky dons shades of goofy glee,
While birds crack jokes from every tree.
In this jest-filled haze, we bask,
Just don't forget to smile and laugh!

With cheerful zest, the day unfolds,
In a punchline of gold, life beholds.
A splash of fun at every bend,
Good morning, sunshine, our silly friend.

Citrus Kisses of the Dawn

Kissed by sunshine's fruity glee,
The dawn has come to tickle thee.
Bright beams like laughter through the trees,
Whispers of joy in the morning breeze.

Silly clouds in a citrus race,
Chasing giggles across the space.
Each giggle is a slice of cheer,
As daybreak dances, far and near.

A playful breeze twirls hats awry,
While squirrels giggle and pass us by.
The sun's a chef with a jester's flair,
Whipping up fun from the vibrant air.

Jokes in the shimmer, laughs galore,
With each tickle, we crave more.
Books of jest write on the skies,
As morning opens with joyful sighs.

Sunlit Citrus Serenade

The sun breaks out in a fruity song,
While the world hums along, oh so strong.
Chirping birds join in the fun,
In a zesty tune 'til the day is done.

Jokes flutter lightly on the breeze,
As morning stirs the yawning trees.
Each leaf a chuckle, bright and spry,
Watch the sun share a wink with the sky.

The vibes are juicy, ripe for the day,
With silly rhymes in a sunny ballet.
Bright ribbons of laughter fill the space,
As golden laughter sets the pace.

The warmth wraps round like a hug so tight,
Making mornings feel just right.
Under the glow of citrus hue,
A serenade rolls sweet and true.

Dawn's Golden Elixir

A golden cup spills morning cheer,
With giggles and grins that draw us near.
As sunlight sips on honeyed light,
The world awakens in pure delight.

Rays like bubbles bounce and play,
Frolicking freely, come what may.
With every beam, a joke is cast,
In this bright brew, mischief's amassed.

Pancakes flip in a sunny spree,
While syrup sings a sweet decree.
The air's alive with fruity puns,
As morning frolics and always runs.

A splash of fun and zest abound,
In laughter, love, and light profound.
With open hearts, we toast the dawn,
To this elixir, we will respond!

A Symphony of Golden Dawn

In the morning light, they play,
The fruits of cheer come out to sway.
A zesty tune fills the bright air,
With every joke, they dance without a care.

A citrus band, they sing and twirl,
As laughter streams and joy unfurl.
Each peel a note in sunlit glee,
A melody of sweet esprit.

Their skins aglow, a glowing sight,
Each joke a burst, oh what delight!
A round of puns in every bite,
The day begins, all feels so right.

With flavors bright, they stand so proud,
In nature's concert, singing loud.
In every laugh, a zestful cheer,
A golden dawn, we hold so dear.

Sunbeams on Citrus Fruit

Beneath the sun, the citruses gleam,
A fruit parade, it feels like a dream.
With jokes about zest, the day ignites,
As giggles and chuckles fill the heights.

The oranges giggle with a smile so wide,
While lemons tumble, taking a ride.
With puns and pips, they join the fun,
Brightly they shine under the sun.

From tangy tales to sweet delight,
The citrus crew keeps spirits bright.
Each burst of laughter, a juicy jest,
In this sunny realm, we feel so blessed.

As playful rays dance on their skin,
In this fruity verse, the joy begins.
With humor ripe, we lift our glass,
Here in the morning, let good times amass.

The Lustrous Dawn's Arrival

When dawn breaks with a citrus grin,
The world awakens, let the fun begin!
With every slice, a joke does sprout,
As laughter rolls the citrus route.

Here comes the twist with a silly flair,
The sun beams down with laughable air.
Each fruit is ripe with quirky charm,
In zesty whim, we sing alarm.

Orange and yellow, baby, don't be shy,
With every smile, we reach for the sky.
The joke is on us, or is it on them?
We smile as bright as the fruit's diadem.

And as the dawn paints the world anew,
We raise a toast to the laugh we pursue.
For every day is a chance to play,
In this citrus world, we find our way.

Citrus Echoes in the Morning

Echoes of laughter fill the mist,
As morning arrives, the fun can't be missed.
Lemonade wishes float in the air,
With giggles and grins, they dance everywhere.

Grapefruits gossip, exchanging their strife,
'Tis better to laugh than savor life!
Each playful jab, a zestful jest,
In this nectarous world, we feel so blessed.

A joyful twist in every song,
Citrus notes, where we all belong.
With pulpy puns and juiced-up cheer,
The dawn breaks forth, let's give a cheer!

So grab a slice and take a bite,
In this funny morn, all feels just right.
With echoes of citrus in the day,
Let's laugh and sing in the sun's array.

Golden Mist on the Horizon

A slice of joy spills from the skies,
As morning unfolds with sunny ties.
Pancakes fail to flip in a silly dance,
Everyone's waiting for breakfast's chance.

The orange clouds giggle with delight,
Making shadows play hide and seek in light.
Birds chirp witty jokes from their perch,
While squirrels serve brunch in their grand church.

The laughter spreads like jam on bread,
While bees wear hats, sprightly and red.
Beneath a canopy of bright, funny hues,
We toast the morning and share our views.

Juicy Rays of Hope

A morning burst, oh what a sight,
With cheerleaders buzzing and feeling light.
The world is fresh, like a wink and a grin,
As laughter bubbles and spills from within.

Toast pops up with a joyful leap,
Families gather, their secrets to keep.
With each silly joke, the sun starts to climb,
We dance like fruit flies, feeling sublime.

The bright rays squeeze out worries and fears,
Painting our smiles like the sunny years.
Citrusy giggles and zesty mirth,
Wrap around our hearts, oh what a birth!

Citrus Lullabies at Dawn

The dawn plays tricks with a zesty hum,
As oranges whisper, 'Here comes the fun!'
Juicy tales flutter in the dawn's embrace,
Each story spritzed with a tangy grace.

Silly squirrels sing to the sleepy leaves,
Tickling the branches where the sunshine weaves.
Kittens chase shadows, their tails on a spree,
In this merry circus, just let it be!

As butter flies dance in the sweetened air,
The giggles of morning fill everywhere.
With zest in our hearts and laughs all around,
The sun drapes its blanket on the waking ground.

Sunrise in a Citrus Grove

In a grove full of giggles, the sun starts to rise,
With lemony whispers and teasing sighs.
A parade of colors on nature's great stage,
The morning unfolds with a comedic page.

The fruit hangs low, like hats on a line,
Wobbling a jig in a dance that's divine.
A rascal of sunshine brushes the leaves,
While bees in bow ties hum sweet little thieves.

Each blossom is chuckling in petals of gold,
Tales of the morning eagerly told.
With laughter like juice, we squeeze every drop,
In the citrusy world where good vibes never stop.

Reflections of Citrus Dreams

In a glass of zest, I see my face,
Waking up with a citrus grace.
Juggling fruits in morning glee,
Sipping sunshine, oh so free.

My cat gives me a curious glance,
As I twirl in my breakfast dance.
With each bright sip, I can't help but smile,
Life's a fruity, fizzy while!

Orange peel confetti in my hair,
I drip and drop, without a care.
The toast pops up, a golden show,
I cheer for crumbs that dare to flow!

So let's toast to this tangy cheer,
And laugh away the syrupy fear.
With every gulp, the giggles rise,
In my silly world, the flavor flies!

Citrus Dawn's Warm Embrace

Here comes the sun, all yellow and bright,
With a twist of citrus, oh what a sight!
My pancakes are flipping, the syrup is thick,
As I dance in the kitchen, with my best fruity trick.

I missed the toast, it flew across the room,
While the juice made my breakfast bloom.
Spinning and slipping, I grab the mug,
It's morning mayhem, and I give it a shrug!

The dog looks puzzled, tilting his head,
As I serenade pancakes instead of bread.
I sing to the jug of squeezed delight,
Making breakfast an absolute flight!

So here's to the chaos, the laughter and fun,
With every citrus hug, the day has begun.
Let's sip on life, with a wink and a cheer,
In the warmth of the morning, nothing to fear!

The Golden Citrus Horizon

A zesty burst to greet the day,
With giggles and rays that seem to play.
I find my socks, but they're not a pair,
As I leap like a fruit with vibrant flair!

The toast gets all tan, it waves like a flag,
While I bounce with joy, it's hard not to brag.
I'll juice up my morning, with spritz and a jive,
In a carnival kitchen, I really come alive!

A squirt of bright juice, the table's a fright,
With oranges rolling into the night.
I laugh at the mess, what a messy fate,
But oh, what a taste, it's worth all the weight!

So here's to the zest, and here's to the fun,
With every round sip, I'm never outdone.
I claim this bright morning, let the laughter ensue,
In this golden patch, I'll dance with you!

A Morning Ripe for Joy

Sunshine spills into my mug,
With a silly dance and a citrus hug.
Eggs are flipping, pancakes parade,
In a carnival kitchen, my worries fade!

The cat joins in, with a playful pounce,
As I twirl with oranges, we bounce and flounce.
Coffee dribbles, an artistic splash,
Creating a masterpiece—oh, what a crash!

Sticky fingers, but that's just fine,
In a splattered world, I'll dine like a swine.
With every burst of joy, I'll cheer,
Pouring bright laughter into my cheer!

The day is fresh, with giggles to spare,
As morning's zest wraps me in care.
So toast to the fun, let's spread some cheer,
In this juicy moment, let's live without fear!

Yellow Skies Unfolding

When the sun pops up, oh what a sight,
Clouds glowing bright, pure delight!
Birds dance like they've had too much drink,
It's morning again, let's give it a wink!

Syrupy sunshine spills on the street,
Pavement's sticky, but oh, what a treat!
Sipping silly joy from a plastic cup,
Chasing the giggles, never give up!

Orange and yellow swirl in a cheer,
Who knew dawn could bring such a jeer?
Each ray of light holds a laugh and a jest,
In this wacky world, we're truly blessed!

With every grin that stretches so wide,
The sky's a canvas, the clouds our guide.
So raise your mug filled with morning zest,
Let's toast to the day, and all of its jest!

Fresh Squeeze of Dawn

The day begins, with a funny twist,
Birds take flight, raise a small fist!
Juicy joy drips from the trees,
Gathering giggles with a soft breeze.

Pineapple pants and orange hats,
Dancing squirrels, imagine that!
Coffee brews, but it's really a potion,
To spark the morning's wild commotion!

Muffins giggle, jam on the side,
Every bite's like a rollercoaster ride.
Sticky fingers and crumbs galore,
Laughter erupts, who could ask for more?

The sun's a clown, with a painted face,
Shining tall, bringing smiles to the place.
Stirring up mischief in warm sunlight,
Let's bounce around, till the stars ignite!

Dewy Citrus Serenade

Dewdrops dance on rooftops awry,
A citrus serenade that tickles the sky.
Every drop's a giggle, a playful tease,
Nature's way of making us sneeze!

Waking up is a grand affair,
With zesty whispers and warm fresh air.
Socks mismatched, what a sight to behold,
In this thrilling jest, we break the mold!

Crickets play trumpets, frogs lead the band,
Sunbeams sway, oh, isn't it grand?
Under this sun, so cheerful and bright,
Let's dance and sing, oh what pure delight!

With every tickle from the morning breeze,
Laughter bubbles up, aiming to please.
Join the fun, let your spirits float,
In this merry world, let's all take note!

Awakening with Zesty Light

Awake and ready for this wild ride,
With a zesty glow to steal your pride.
Frothy bubbles in the morning cup,
Time to jump in, let's erupt!

Citrus giggles twirl through the air,
How can a day start without flair?
Napping cats are plotting a scheme,
To snatch our breakfast, it seems like a dream!

Golden rays tickle every tree,
Jokes abound, as bright as can be.
Sun in our eyes, laughter on lips,
With every sip, let's do backflips!

As the world spins in fruity delight,
Let's gather the joy, all through the night.
A catchy tune plays in our hearts,
With every laugh, our adventure starts!

Golden Rays on Zesty Leaves

Morning beams dance on dew-drenched greens,
A toast to the quirks that nature intervenes.
Bumblebees buzzing with comedic twirls,
As they flirt with flowers and twirl into swirls.

Birds chirp with laughter, they sing silly tunes,
While sunbeams frolic like playful raccoons.
Each leaf gleams bright, a jester in cheer,
Nature's own party, let's join in the sneer.

Joyful moments sizzle, like pans in a play,
Dish out the giggles, they brighten the day.
So let's squeeze laughter from this citrus spree,
And roll in the rays, wild and carefree.

Here comes the sun, with a wink and a grin,
Turning the morning into a lively din.
In this zesty realm, let worries be few,
Dance with the light, let joy shine through.

Morning Melodies of Citric Bliss

Whimsical whiffs of oranges afloat,
With grapefruit giggles, they put on a coat.
A parrot in pajamas starts chirping a tune,
While lemons in line play the tune of a croon.

Slicing through laughter, the day comes alive,
Fruits in the garden put on a wild jive.
Quick-stepping radishes dip in the grass,
While peppery carrots bring comic sass.

The sun spills like juice from a clumsy cup,
As shadows do tango, they wiggle and sup.
With pep in their steps, greens all align,
Holding a conference on how to have fun.

Each moment is jolly, a playful delight,
As fruits start to mingle from morning 'til night.
Let's peel back the layers of laughter and zest,
In this joyful garden, we're clearly the best.

A Citrus Morn's Promise

Bouncing out of bed, the sun's burst of scope,
With dreams laced in citrus, we dance and we hope.
The kettle's a comedian, steaming with flair,
While toast joins the banter, all buttered with care.

A playful pastry sings songs of the morn,
As sweet as a joke made by a jolly corn.
Jams laugh and giggle in jars on the shelf,
While muffins tease croissants, "You're just not myself!"

Butterflies flutter, a comedic flight,
Giving props to the flowers, what a glorious sight.
In this zesty bazaar, let laughter ignite,
As the day sprouts a grin, basking in light.

With a wink from the sun, the world starts to play,
A silly adventure leads us on our way.
So grab your zest and let joy be your guide,
In this vibrant morn, let happiness ride.

The Spice of Distant Sunlight

Quesadillas chat while teetering high,
With beans that chuckle when sunlight's awry.
Pineapples gossip, their tales intertwined,
As jalapeños giggle with a hot, fruity mind.

Cucumbers roll in on a vine of delight,
Wrestling zucchinis in an epic daylight.
Tomatoes, red-faced, spill secrets of flair,
While carrots on swings float through cool morning air.

The distant sun's rays are up to their tricks,
Tickling each veggie, oh, what a mix!
Lettuce joins in, with its crisp-hued applause,
Waving its leaves to the jester's grand cause.

So here's to the laughter, the spice, and the fun,
In gardens of mirth, till the day is all done.
As sunlight adorns with its golden embrace,
Every giggle and grin is a bright, sunny face.

www.ingramcontent.com/pod-product-compliance
Lightning Source LLC
Chambersburg PA
CBHW051731290426
43661CB00122B/232